TURKEY

TURKEY

Photographs by
ROLAND AND SABRINA MICHAUD

Introduction by
DANIEL FARSON

83 plates in colour

THAMES AND HUDSON

Any copy of this book issued by the publisher as a paperback
is sold subject to the condition that it shall not
by way of trade or otherwise be lent, resold, hired out or
otherwise circulated without the publisher's prior consent
in any form of binding or cover other than that in which
it is published and without a similar condition including
these words being imposed on a subsequent purchaser.

Printed and bound in Japan by Dai Nippon

Introduction by Daniel Farson

An Infinite Variety

There are few sights in the world which give me such a sense of exhilaration as the skyline of Istanbul, with that magical combination of curved mosques and slender, pointed minarets, the one enhancing the other – the incomparable panorama celebrated in the opening photographs of this book. When you look across the Golden Horn you realize you are somewhere different.

In fact you are not looking across from Europe to Asia, as you do in the Bosphorus, for the Golden Horn is little more than an inlet, and in spite of the brilliance of the name, it is a dirty one too. The water is black with pollution, though this does not discourage the fishermen who dangle their hooks off Galata Bridge with startling success; and if you go to Pierre Loti's house today and sit outside for a glass of tea, the source of the Golden Horn may look industrial, but there is still the unmistakable realization that you have travelled to a city that remains unique. At the far end of the Golden Horn, the Topkapi Palace is the most remarkable sight of all – a city within the city where life must have been cruel, claustrophobic and magnificent. Yet the image which gives the greatest pleasure is simply the bustle of the water-traffic on the Horn itself, with the New Mosque or Yeni Cami, completed in 1663, at the other end of Galata Bridge if you look across from Pera to old Stamboul. See this on a winter morning, and the tones of grey and pink are so subtle they resemble the smudges of a watercolour painting, as the late-rising sun casts its first reflections on the shimmering water.

How exciting it must have been to cross Europe in the last century on the Orient Express direct to Constantinople, to be carried by sedan chair from the station to the Pera Pelas Oteli, which was built especially to accommodate the passengers. You can stay in this venerable hotel today, with glass cabinets which contain the china used on those early trains, and a wrought-iron lift which ascends with an old-world grace to the spacious rooms above. From here you can walk down the hill to the market between the bridges where glistening fish are displayed in large circular baskets as prettily as sweets in silver paper; or turn in the other direction to the busy main road which leads to the centre of Taksim Square, past the inconspicuous entrance to Flower Sellers' Alley which provides the liveliest night life in Istanbul, with music and dancing, and even acrobats performing at the separate tables on either side of this narrow pathway, overlooked by grey and shuttered houses with cats crouching furtively on the corrugated-iron sheets which protect the people below from falling masonry. When a fight breaks out the waiters whisk the plates from the tables, but it is over in a matter of seconds, and the singing and good humour resume as if there had been no interruption.

How wasteful it would be to go to Istanbul and fail to see the famous landmarks revealed in these photographs: the Blue Mosque and the interior of the Hagia Sophia; the great mosques built by the architect Sinan for the Ottoman sultans in the sixteenth century; the exquisite tile-decorations of the Rüstem Pasha Mosque; the Byzantine mosaics of a former church, the Kariye Camii; the stupendous range of rooftops of Topakapi with the Bosphorus beyond.

Ultimately, however, the charm of a great city lies in the details which form the whole, like the gracious squares of London or the narrow streets of Paris. Parts of Istanbul are dark and dirty, but there is constant surprise around the corner, especially if you explore the shoreline of the Bosphorus.

You can find palaces here as well, though they might belong to a different country. In contrast to the Eastern romance of the sultans' Topkapi with its Harem and labyrinthine passages, there is the Dolmabahçe Palace, of Western splendour, which lies near the great bridge which spans the two continents. This is a fantasy sugar-cake from the outside, in a style that could be described as Italian-Baroque. Inside, there is a dash of Indian, with ivory tusks sent by foreign potentates, and a glass chandelier, presented to the Sultan Abdul Aziz by Queen Victoria, which weighs four and a half tons. With most of the furniture on this same gigantic scale, it seems as if every detail has been enlarged out of all proportion to emphasize the puniness of man. Dolmabahçe was built in the mid-nineteenth century with the deliberate aim of moving away from old traditions to a new style which would be more acceptable to western visitors, unaware that these were enthralled by exotic mysteries of the East. This was the last home of the sultans, but the Palace acquired a new fame as the official residence of the first Turkish President, Kemal Atatürk, who died here on the morning of 10 November 1938. Today the ferry-boats on the Bosphorus outside sound their hooters at the hour of his death.

On the Asian side opposite, the Beylerbey Palace is miniature by comparison, built as a summer retreat for Abdul Aziz, and the final resting-place for Abdul Hamit II, the last autocratic sultan of the Ottoman Empire, who died here in 1918 as a virtual prisoner.

Another backward glance to the days of the Turkish sultans can be gained on a visit to the Naval Museum (near the Dolmabahçe) where you can see replicas of the galleys which look so splendid in prints of old Constantinople, complete with figures of the oarsmen and the sultans themselves. Alongside them is the simple rowboat so small it might have been a child's, beautifully carved out of hardwood especially for Atatürk, as different from one of these immense galleys as you can imagine.

Most cities have changed out of all recognition in the twentieth century and usually for the worse, but Istanbul retains the charm of Constantinople. In 1718 the English explorer Lady Mary Wortley Montagu wrote to Lady Bristol of her journey down the Bosphorus of twenty miles, describing 'the most Beautiful variety of Prospects . . . the Asian side is covered with fruit trees, villages and the most delightful landscapes in Nature. On the European side stands Constantinople . . . an agreeable mix of Gardens, Pine and Cypress trees, Palaces, Mosques and publick buildings rais'd one above the other . . .'

This description stands today, with the last of the grand old wooden mansions dotted along the shoreline, and the village of Tarabia still used as an exclusive summer resort. This is where the foreign embassies retired in the heat of summer, and the sense of luxury is maintained by the scores of excellent restaurants along this stretch. You can stop by chance at one where the water laps against the balcony whenever a ferry stops at the landing-stage, or go to the grander restaurants which are famous for their seafood. Inland you will find the simpler *lokanta*, and the difference is best explained by this anecdote: a customer ate in his favourite *lokanta* every day until he was called away on business. Returning a few months later, he was dismayed by the startling difference in his bill, and asked what had happened. 'When you were here last,' the proprietor informed him proudly, 'we were a *lokanta*. Now we are a restaurant!'

Turkish Cuisine

Why is Turkish food so good? The maitre d'hotel at the Divan in Istanbul insists that Turkish cuisine is the best in the world after French and Russian. To appreciate the scope of Turkish cuisine one has to remember the range of the Ottoman Empire, which stretched from the Middle East to North Africa, bringing paprika to Hungary and coffee to the gates of Vienna. Many of the finest dishes derived from the Caucasus, like *cerkes tavugu* – pieces of chicken pounded together with walnuts – prepared for the sultan by the Circassian girls in his Harem, apparently the most beautiful of all as well as being marvellous cooks. There is another speciality which I find irresistible, especially when eaten in the open air, washed down by a cool white wine like Villa Doluca or Kavak. These are deep-fried pastries filled with cheese and spinach, or sometimes meat, rolled up like a cigar – hence *sigara boregi* (or *borek*). These are hot appetisers to complement the dishes of cold *mezes* which introduce every meal and typify all that is best in Turkish food. If you relish the taste of olive oil, yoghurt, garlic and aubergine, you will find that the wide selection of *mezes*, enhanced by herbs and spices, provides a meal in itself. There are stuffed vine-leaves and stuffed green peppers, and a braised aubergine known as *imam bayildi*, which means 'the priest fainted' – on being presented with something so delicious.

Though Turkey covers a vast area of land, the surrounding waters are as vital as to any island, and a sideboard at Facyo's displayed the range of seafood taken from the neighbouring seas: palamut from the Black Sea; red mullet, mussels and clams from the Bosphorus; bass from the Sea of Marmara; swordfish from the Mediterranean; and giant prawns from Iskenderun to the far south.

Looking outside at the massive Soviet tankers which dwarf the busy traffic of the Bosphorus, one can almost sense the frustration of the Russian captains who are forced to sail this gauntlet. What a close-run thing it was in the 1914-18 war when the Allied ships failed to push forward after they entered the straits of the Dardanelles, into the Sea of Marmara beyond. With Constantinople in disarray, the British might have captured the city without a shot fired and changed the course of the war, and Russia, in return for her support of the Allied cause, would have become the new master of the Bosphorus.

Most defeats are surrounded by a barrage of excuses made with hindsight, and in this Gallipoli excels. The British hesitated, and the Turks seized their opportunity to consolidate their positions. Even so, the Allied troops were within yards and minutes of victory on the first landing, and might have succeeded if it had not been for the presence of the right man at the right spot at the right moment – Mustafa Kemal, later known as Kemal Attatürk. This extraordinary man is one of the great leaders of the twentieth century, and as you travel through Turkey there is not a village square that does not boast a statue in his honour today.

The Black Sea

There must be waterways which are just as impressive – I remember sailing up the St Lawrence river when I was a boy, and crossing the Panama Canal later – but the Bosphorus has a jauntiness which is irresistible if you observe the changing scene from the decks of a Turkish passenger-ship like the *Izmir*, especially when you know that you have several days of sailing along the Black Sea coast ahead of you. Ports like Sinop and Giresun are off the tourist track and remain refreshingly unspoilt, though Trabzon is no longer the romantic place evoked by Rose Macaulay in *The Towers of Trebizond*: 'Still the towers of Trebizond, the fabled city, shimmer on a far horizon, gated and walled and held in luminous enchantment.' The towers today are those of a flour-mill and industrial chimneys, but the enchantment returns once you are inside the town, with the old walled city on a ridge between two ravines suggesting that the ancient name of Trapezus was derived from the trapeze. The Hotel Ozgur overlooks a large main square with trees ranging from palms to pines and a statue of Atatürk flanked by beds of red flowers. The Church of Hagia Sophia above, which was built in 1250, conveys the splendour of the past, when the city was a Byzantine fortress for two hundred and fifty years, the last Christian outpost after the fall of Constantinople, surviving for eight further years until it was besieged by Sultan Mehmet II in 1461. A modern attraction is the white-washed chalet presented by the grateful citizens to Kemal Atatürk, whose portraits decorate the rooms inside, regarded with silent awe by peasant women wearing headscarves and grave young soldiers with shaven heads, all paying their respects to the first President of the Turkish Republic. It is a simple place with a pleasing atmosphere.

Sumela

'East is East and West is West, but Turkey is something different.' This was said proudly by a Turk, and the claim is true. Turkey has the variety of a continent rather than a country. Drive along the coast from Trabzon to Rize and look out from the Botanical Gardens at the top over the hills which are lined with terraces and tea-plants (most of Turkey's tea is grown here) and you might be in Sri Lanka. Travel inland, and you enter the Turkish 'Alps', a country of deep green valleys dotted with chalets and grazing cows very like those of Switzerland and Austria, except that the focal point of the distant villages is a rising minaret rather than the steeple of a church. There are several astonishing monasteries south of Trabzon, and that of Sumela is hardly discernible at first, perched on a distant mountain-ledge between the branches of trees in the foreground noted for their different shades of green. If you climb the track to Sumela's façade, which looks as if it has been painted on the cliff-face nearly four thousand feet high, you might feel disappointed to find it in such a state of disrepair; but this first reaction is replaced by admiration. The place must have been sublime, secure in its solitude and safe from attack, which is why it was chosen in the first place, despite the legend that a Greek monk saw it in a vision and sailed from Athens in AD 385. Today the doors and windows are gaping holes, and visitors have scratched their names on the frescoes in the church in their pathetic hope of immortality, yet this was once a centre of civilization, with three chapels, dormitories and courtyards, and a library that was world-famous for its thousands of books in the fifteenth century. Considered as a fortress for *tranquillity*, Sumela is deeply moving.

Priene and Aphrodisias

To travel through Turkey without a sense of history would be as wasteful as crossing it by train with the blinds pulled down. The combination of present beauty and past splendour is unsurpassed, even by Greece, with the added excitement that many of the ancient sites have yet to be fully excavated. The thrill of discovery remains, with the chance of climbing to the ruined city above the miles of empty beach at Patara to find the theatre half-covered by sand-dunes, or of mooring at the island of Gemile, near Fethiye, to stumble, literally, on ruins yet to be explored by archaeologists. Moments like these remain stamped on the memory. The restoration of Ephesus is a remarkable achievement, worthy of one of the Seven Wonders of the ancient world, for it was the greatest city in Asia under Roman rule with a population of three hundred thousand; yet there is even greater reward in visiting Priene at the honeyed hour before dusk, when the light enhances the stone, revealing colours which are killed by the mid-day glare. Once this was a hillside port which welcomed Alexander when he freed the territory from the Persians, but the water has receded so far that Priene overlooks a plain. The ruins are modest compared to those at Ephesus, but the simplicity of the five Ionian columns, part of the Temple of Athena designed for Alexander, is a vivid pleasure.

Further inland, an uncomfortable distance away from the cruise ships of Kuşadasi, lies the archaeological site of Aphrodisias, which may surpass even that of Ephesus when it is fully revealed, and stands comparison already. Looking down on the theatre it is hard to believe that this area was concealed by a village only a few years ago. In contrast to the stadium, one of the largest in the world where thirty thousand spectators watched chariot races and cheered the gladiators, or the ample theatre which looks across the plateau to the marble quarries in the hills of Baba Dağ, the odeon is minuscule, intimate and enclosed, with a mere four hundred seats for the most distinguished members of the city, who relaxed in the comfort of marble chairs with arms. This was the peaceful setting, surrounded by trees, where music was played on flutes and lyres by an orchestra on the sunken stage, sometimes occupied by a philosopher who read his latest work to the select audience, while slaves waited with rolls of papyrus to record copies, using an ink made from resin, soot, wine-dregs and cuttlefish. Remains of the statues and decorations which enhanced the odeon can be seen in the museum today and confirm the grace of the life enjoyed by the citizens a thousand years ago. With the significant absence of prisons and army barracks, the impression is given of a truly civilized community, and it is possible to people it in imagination after you have absorbed the atmosphere: the elders in their togas discussing the issues of the day, the avenues filled with citizens going about their business, children on their way to school, athletes going to the sports grounds, others making their way to market where the air is rent by the din of the smith's hammer and sculptor's chisel, the cries of the merchants selling their wares, and the modulated voices of the story-tellers. At night the city was lit by torches and lamps, and the audience at the theatre would laugh at the latest comedy by Plautus, performed by masked actors, while others passed the time sprawled on couches drinking the sweet local wine poured from amphorae by their attendant slaves.

Termessus

If Aphrodisias conveys the grace of that early civilization, then the wilder ruined city of Termessus conveys the strength of it. I was taken there by Ibrahim Buyuk-beni, the doyen of guides though he is now retired, on my first day in Antalya. The road climbs into the mountains twenty miles inland, becoming increasingly alpine in appearance apart from the tortoises which make their laborious way across it. After you stop at a clearing in the pine trees, you walk for a further half-hour until you reach the ruins. You find there the rarest of qualities today: silence and solitude. A theatre overlooks the valley below, perched like an eagle's nest. A smaller odeon was once covered by a roof of red and black marble. There were twenty temples; and you can see the ruins of the gymnasium and the hot baths where the athletes washed off the sand and oil. More unusual are the three containers, the size of small houses, where the Termessians stored their olive oil and even chanelled it down to Antalya by a series of pipelines. But the most remarkable feature of the city was the necropolis in the heart of it, with ten thousand tombs which tumble down the mountainside today much as the earthquake left them in the fifth century. Many are decorated with medusa-heads, lions and griffons, and the disc-like shields which symbolized the strength of the people who lived here. What men they must have been! It is claimed that Termessus was the one place which Alexander failed to conquer when he came here in 333 BC from his winter headquarters at Phaselis, further up the coast. When he rode into the horseshoe valley the Termessians released gigantic nets filled with boulders which cascaded on the men below, injuring Alexander's horse and killing a number of his soldiers. With the scornful excuse that he could not be bothered to start a protracted seige of such an insignificant stronghold, he rode away, setting fire to the precious olive groves as he did so.

Cappadocia

There cannot be many landscapes as weird and wonderful as that of Cappadocia. It looks as if the earth was thrown up in a great upheaval and then froze just as it was starting to melt from an overwhelming heat. And this is roughly what *did* happen. The volcano of Mount Ercyers, which is now extinct, erupted thousands of years ago covering the area with lava which stiffened into pumice and tufa stone. Then the erosion of wind and rain, like sculptors, moulded the shape of the conical towers we see today. But this is more than a marvellous freak of nature; it has the interest of the man-made as well, for it is with astonishment, even a sense of shock, that you observe that the holes in the rocks are windows and doors carved out by people, who have lived here since 3000 BC. Pumice is easy to mould, for it hardens only when it is exposed to the air, so these rock faces provided natural homes in a district which is otherwise bleak and inhospitable. Even now the caves are used as coolers for fruit, which can be stored for months and remain preserved. The honeycomb cliffs at Zelve were inhabited until 1950 when the people were evacuated because their cavernous homes were no longer safe.

The size and scope of the area is staggering. It needs time to absorb the complexity and the details of this Early Christian settlement, with the rock churches, most of which are richly decorated with frescoes, like that of the Last Supper – a massive fish resting on a dish surrounded by Christ and the Apostles – which brightens the Dark Church, Karanlík Kilisse. As you drive through this bizarre landscape, from Ürgüp to Göreme, there is constant surprise. Yet, there is even more here than meets the eye: an underground civilization, which surpassed the troglodyte community above, created vast subterranean cities where the Christians descended when the Arabs invaded from the East, connecting several levels with a labyrinth of passages. At their peak around the seventh century the population was estimated at over thirty thousand people, which explains the need for ventilator shafts and water-tanks as well as churches. Derinkuyu, which is twenty-nine kilometres south of Nevşehir, has seven stories, reaching to a depth of thirty-five metres; while Kaymaklí, which is connected to Derinkuyu by several kilometres of tunnel, had halls, kitchens, cisterns, wine vats and chapels, making it probably the grandest Christian centre of catacombs in the world. Yet it must have been like Hell once the inhabitants had sealed themselves in by rolling gigantic millstones against the entrance, though no fire was allowed in case any smoke led to their discovery. Crouching along the narrow tunnels, even for a few minutes, gave me an unbearable sense of claustrophobia. The feeling of suffocation must have been appalling, almost outweighing the fear of rape and pillage in the open air above. This extraordinary existence continued until the Seljuk Turks occupied the territory in the eleventh century, leaving the Christian communities in peace at last.

Mount Nemrut

Again it is the imposition of man on the landscape which is so admirable. What effort must have been required to build those cities below the earth and to carve out homes in the rocks above. This is why the great stone figures on Mount Nemrut are so enthralling: they are an act of monumental vanity. This colossal tribute to himself is the work of a single man, though it must have needed an army of ant-like slaves to fulfil it. Presumably Antiochus I of Commagene regarded this as his divine right, for he was descended from Alexander the Great on his mother's side, and from Darius I of Persia on his father's. His statues are four or five times lifesize, a combination of Greek and Persian gods, and sat in a row above a sacrificial altar. Between the statues to Hercules and Zeus, Antiochus built one to himself: 'I, Antiochus, caused this momument to be erected in commemoration of my own glory and that of the gods.' After the battering by wind and rain over two thousand years, the statues are headless now, though the heads have been hoisted upright and look as if they have stood there since the start of time. Only the head of the Goddess of Fortune, adorned with fruit, lies sprawled on the ground, for this was the last to fall, decapitated in a violent thunderstorm as recently as 1962.

For centuries the statues were forgotten until shepherds described them to a German archaeologist who came to the region at the start of the last century. Then a few visitors made their way up the mountainside laboriously by mule. Even now, the road is covered by snow for most of the year, and you have to climb the last part over slippery shale which is treacherous in the darkness shortly before dawn. This, however, is the moment to arrive, though I was unprepared for the force of the wind as I sheltered behind Zeus. Gradually the outlines of the heads emerge, with a tumulus rising like a pyramid behind, a sepulchral mound which might contain the tomb of Antiochus himself, though every attempt to find an entrance has been thwarted by the trembling stones which threaten a landslide at the first thrust of excavation. The scene is more tremendous than I had dared to hope. The bearded Zeus is taller than a man, perhaps the largest sculpted head in the world after those in Easter Island. Stone eagles and lions keep guard, and one magnificent, open-mouthed lion seems to be howling his defiance. The wait for the sun to rise seemed interminable, but gradually it began to lighten, and I could see the endless panorama below me unfold, with the faint ribbon of the Euphrates meandering into the distance. How odd to realize that I was looking down on Mesopotamia, once a fruitful plain, and soon to be transformed again by another man-made wonder, when a vast irrigation scheme diverts the Euphrates and the Tigris, creating a dam and reservoir large enough to alter the climate. No wonder that Antiochus chose such an eminence for his celebration of himself, with blocks of white marble for his statues carried from Gerger thirty kilometres away.

And then the thin light gave way, as the sun came up. It was neither black nor green, as people had insisted, but a raw red force bubbling out of the earth as if the core had been shattered. I was only surprised that I could not *hear* it throb as well as witness this explosion, as powerful as the blast from a furnace door. If a man had never seen the sun rise before, he would fall on his knees at such a sight, in terror of what might follow. Suddenly, the creation by Antiochus was understandable, for this was beyond vanity, despite his boast that 'no living human being shall be able to build anything higher than this shrine.' 'What I have done,' he proclaimed,' 'is proof of my belief in the presence of the gods.' The sun tore itself away from the earth in a matter of seconds, rising paler into the sky, and I was left for a few ecstatic moments shaking with excitement in the violent wind.

Lake Van

Though I have enjoyed travelling by the superlative bus service throughout Turkey, I remember two journeys with particular pleasure: the boat I took from Istanbul to Trabzon, and the train from Istanbul to Lake Van in the east. This has an excellent beginning if you catch the ferry near Galata Bridge and sail out of the Golden Horn to Üsküdar on the opposite side, where the boat moors beside the steps to the station of Haydarpasha Gari. There is a sense of elation as the train leaves Istanbul and you have the chance of seeing the country's back door rather than the touristic façade. We sped past the familiar sights of boys playing football in the early evening, then the houses dwindled, and we entered open country. I unpacked in my comfortable cabin, with bunk and wash-basin, with the satisfaction of knowing that I was travelling to the end of the line, and headed for the buffet car in the next carriage, which may have been modest but served surprising meals, usually delicious, with the unexpected courtesy of a vase of wild flowers picked by the waiters from the surrounding fields during a stop. After two days we crossed a plateau where the only signs of life were the black nomadic tents and flocks of sheep, until we started to climb into the mountains, before the final descent to Tatvan, by the lake, where you transfer to a boat. The lake is the largest in Turkey, the size of Lake Geneva, and there is a strange sense of sailing into limbo if you travel in the darkness, as I did. The lake is so wide that one might be at sea, without a friendly flickering light in sight, nor was there any dining-car or bar to relieve the tedium for the few of us on board, only a snowy television set transmitting an American comedy, which seemed bizarre in the circumstances. It reminded me of those stories in which a group of ill-assorted passengers are thrown together only to realize that they are dead. And far from offering the welcome of a lakeside resort to the traveller arriving at midnight, the town of Van lies inland, though it proved an unpretentious outpost with a charm that grows on one, and is surrounded by some of the most splendid scenery in Turkey.

The small island of Akhtamar is exceptionally lovely, with the old Armenian church with wild flowers in the foreground and the snow-capped mountains on the mainland beyond. The carvings on the outside of the church are unlike anything I had seen before; they are of biblical scenes which reminded us that Armenia was founded in the province of Van by a descendant of Noah. Crossing a plain afterwards, on the opposite shore, we were joined by a pack of snarling dogs which raced beside the car. I was relieved when we left them behind and reached one of the marvels of the region: the source of the Waters of Semiramis, Şemiran Suyu, the irrigation canal built by King Menua when this was the most powerful state in Asia, nearly a thousand years before the birth of Christ. As the canal stretched to Van, fifty-five kilometres away, this was a memorable early feat of construction. Seldom have I felt such a sense of absolute purity, for the waters gush upwards from the rocks at the foot of the hillside like a fountain, in a scene so quietly pastoral that it was easy to understand how people who lived here, closely dependent on the seasons, might believe in the miracles recorded in the Bible, especially with the reality of Lake Van in flood and the constant danger of earthquakes.

The sense of fairy-tale continues with the fortress of Hoşap Kale in the mountainous region on the way to the Iran-Iraq borders, nearly sixty kilometres from Van. The crenelated battlements fulfill a childhood fantasy, with seven observation towers perched on the surrounding hills. One can look down upon it from one of the open archways, and there is still enough activity below to suggest the busy settlement this must have been, up to the 1914-18 war when eight thousand people lived there. An elegant double-arched bridge of black and white stone, built in 1500, spans the river below. Then, commanding the Silk Road, there is the 'Arabian Nights' feudal palace of Ishak Pasha near Doğubayazit, apparently floating on the plain below Mount Ararat – one of the magical sights of the world.

Turkey and the Turks

The photographs by Roland and Sabrina Michaud illustrate the most interesting places to be seen in Turkey today: Cappadocia and the stone heads on Mount Nemrut, the frozen calcium waterfalls of Pamukkale and the beehive huts of Harran near the Syrian border, once the ancient city of Charan, mentioned in Genesis. But marvellous though these sites are, with that incomparable coastline from Alyana to Bodrum, Turkey would be lifeless without the Turks. Nearly all our preconceptions about Turkey are the opposite of the truth – we think of a hard and barren country, yet the overwhelming impression is that of greenery, apart from the central plains, from the twenty-six shades of green in the woods at Sumela to the pine-clad fjords as you enter Marmaris. Equally the Turks are thought of as hard people, which may be true in terms of strength, but this impression is belied the moment that faces are transformed by smiles. Then comes the welcome, and the surprising discovery that the Turks have a strong sense of humour which relishes the ridiculous. The Turks are the best of friends, and any traveller will confirm that Turkish hospitality is something scarcely known in the Western world today. Quite literally, you are considered 'a visitor from God'. I have been welcomed by a rich family at their house near Gümüşhane, a splendid old wooden house to which its owners return once a year from their other home in Tarabia – the annual event for their elderly caretaker, whose eyes were bright with excitement and whose hands were stained from the juice of walnuts he had been collecting in the orchard outside. The rest of his year is spent looking after the family's property and preparing for their visit by chopping firewood, attending to the beehives, and picking the fruit for the home-made jams – apricot, plum, cherry, and rose-petal – which were offered to me for breakfast the next morning with the cool, sharp taste of yoghurt. The old man reminded me of Firs in *The Cherry Orchard*, and this is as close as I shall ever get to the nineteenth-century world of Chekhov.

Just as memorable was the time I got lost in my search for the tomb of the Fearless King in the hills above Silifke, when a peasant invited me into his hut, a stone block with rough wooden steps up to the roof and an encampment of outhouses covered by a black material which made them look nomadic. Inside, the room was blessedly cool and scrupulously clean, with a tier of beds at the end where the entire family slept one above the other at night. I removed my shoes and sat on broad pillows laid out for my benefit, and a banquet gradually appeared, instead of the cup of *chai* I had been expecting. First and most welcome of all was a gleaming jug with cold water; then apples, bread as thin as tissue paper to enfold the shirred eggs presented on a dish, and bowls of yoghurt, all served on large circular tin trays. And, finally, the tea.

The women served us but stayed in the background where they watched the scene eagerly, and the old man's sons sat behind their father respectfully, but refused to smoke in front of him. On such occasions there is no question of payment; that would be insulting to Turkish generosity.

Today, I have as many friends in Turkey as in my own country, and they are friends for life. The magnificent photographs by Roland and Sabrina Michaud present the people as well as the places: the wrestlers and Whirling Dervishes, a shepherdess in Cappadocia, children playing in Ankara. Those who have never been to Turkey can travel vicariously through these pages and may be encouraged to see the country for themselves; for those who know and love Turkey as I do, these photographs will bring the happiest of memories flooding back, with a new resolve to return.

Map of Turkey showing locations mentioned in the Introduction and plate captions

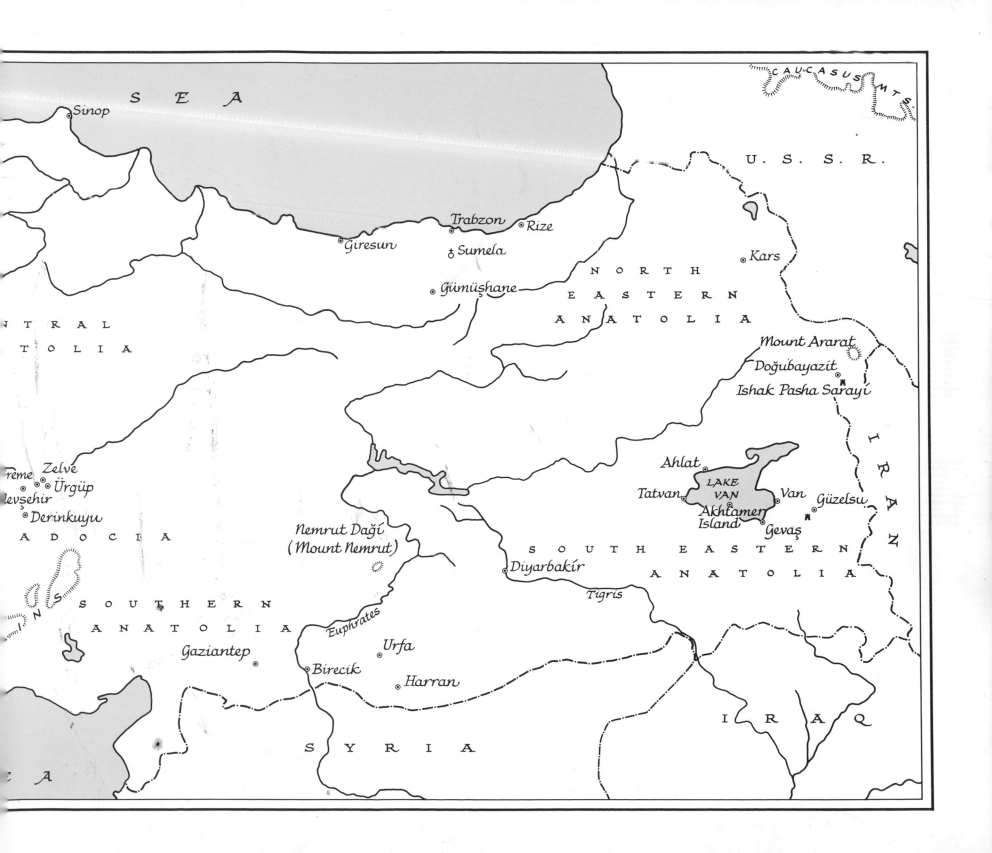

List of plates

1

2

3

9-12

15

16

17

19

21   22

23

24

27   28

29   30

41 42

47

48

49   50

53

54

55

57

58

63

64

67

71

72

73

77   78

79

80

83